BY JOSEPH RODMAN DRAKE.

ILLUSTRATED FROM ORIGINAL DRAWINGS BY F. O. C. DARLEY.

ILLUMINATED COVER BY JOHN A. HOWS.

Music from Bellini, by Geo. Danskin.

NEW YORK:
JAMES G. GREGORY, NO. 46 WALKER STREET.
1861.

BY JOSEPH RODMAN DRAKE.

I.

When Freedom from her mountain height
  Unfurled her standard to the air,
She tore the azure robe of night,
  And set the stars of glory there.
She mingled with its gorgeous dyes
The milky baldric of the skies,
And striped its pure celestial white
With streakings of the morning light;
Then from his mansion in the sun
She called her eagle-bearer down,
And gave into his mighty hand
The symbol of her chosen land.

II.

Majestic monarch of the cloud,
  Who rear'st aloft thy regal form
To hear the tempest-trumpings loud,
  And see the lightning-lances driven,
When stride the warriors of the storm,
And rolls the thunder-drum of heaven!
Child of the sun! to thee 'tis given
  To guard the banner of the free!
To hover in the sulphur smoke,
To ward away the battle stroke,
And bid its blendings shine afar,
Like rainbows on the cloud of war—
  The harbingers of victory!

III.

Flag of the brave! thy folds shall fly,
The sign of hope and triumph high;
When speaks the trumpet's signal tone,
And the long line comes gleaming on,
Ere yet the life-blood, warm and wet,
Has dimm'd the glistening bayonet,
Each soldier's eye shall brightly turn
To where thy sky-born glories burn;
And as his springing steps advance,
Catch war and vengeance from the glance:
And when the cannon-mouthings loud
Heave in wild wreaths the battle-shroud,
And gory sabres rise and fall
Like shoots of flame on midnight's pall—
  Then shall thy meteor-glances glow,
And cowering foes shall sink beneath
  Each gallant arm that strikes below
That lovely messenger of death!

IV.

Flag of the seas! on ocean's wave,
Thy stars shall glitter o'er the brave;
When death, careering on the gale,
Sweeps darkly round the bellied sail,
And frighted waves rush wildly back
Before the broadside's reeling rack,
Each dying wanderer of the sea
Shall look at once to heaven and thee,
And smile to see thy splendors fly
In triumph o'er his closing eye!
  Flag of the free heart's hope and home,
By angel hands to valor given,
  Thy stars have lit the welkin dome,
And all thy hues were born in heaven!
  Forever float that standard sheet
Where breathes the foe that falls before us,
  With Freedom's soil beneath our feet,
And Freedom's banner streaming o'er us!

The American Flag.

Words by J. R. DRAKE. Music by BELLINI.

Arranged by GEO. DANSKIN.

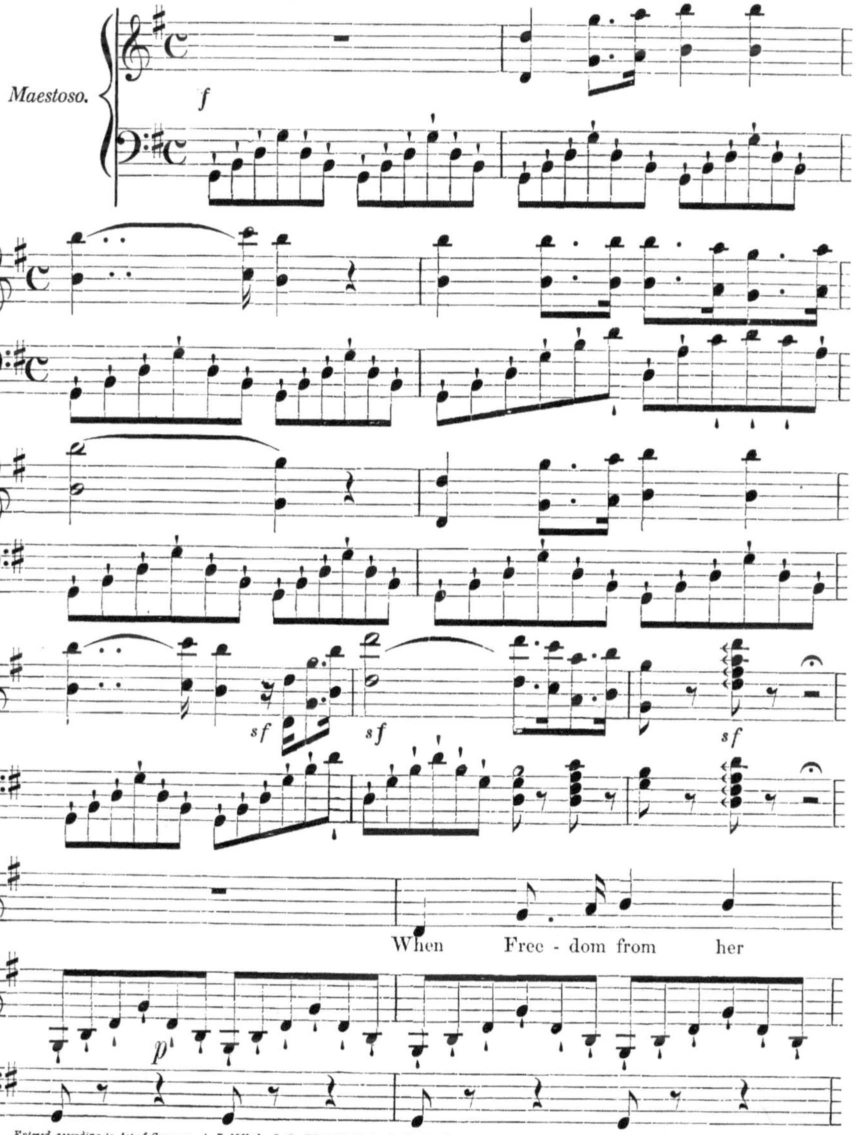
Maestoso.
f
sf
sf
sf
p
When Free - dom from her

moun - - tain height, Un - furl'd her stan - dard to the
air, ... She tore the a - zure
robe of night, And set the stars . . . . of glo - ry
there. She min - gled with its
f
p

gor - geous dies, The mil - ky bal - dric
of the skies, And striped its . . . . pure ce - - - -
- les tial white, With streak - ings from the
morn-ing light; Then from her man - sion in the sun, She

call'd her Ea - gle bear - er down, ...
And gave in - to his migh - ty hand, The symbol
cres
of . . . . her cho - sen land
f
cres
ff

PUBLICATIONS FOR THE TIMES.

I.

THE STAR SPANGLED BANNER:

ILLUSTRATED FROM DRAWINGS BY F. O. C. DARLEY.

The Publisher has now ready a beautiful parlor-table edition of "THE STAR SPANGLED BANNER," exquisitely Illustrated by F. O. C. DARLEY, with an Illuminated Cover by JOHN A. HOWS, containing the Music, arranged by Francis H. Brown.

This beautiful edition of our popular National Song is sold, with the Illustrations, at the ordinary price of the music alone, and is welcomed by all as an elegant and timely issue. Quarto. Price, 25 cents.

II.

THE GREAT ISSUES BEFORE THE COUNTRY:

AN ORATION, BY EDWARD EVERETT.

DELIVERED AT THE NEW YORK ACADEMY OF MUSIC, JULY 4TH, 1861.

The most masterly and exhaustive statement of the issues before the country which has yet been made. 12mo. 48 pp. Price, 15 cents.

III.

THE CAUSES OF THE CIVIL WAR:

BY JOHN LOTHROP MOTLEY, LL.D., D.C.L.,

Author of "The Rise of the Dutch Republic," and "History of the United Netherlands." 12mo. 40 pp. Uniform with "Everett's Oration." Price, 10 cents.

IV.

THE FALLACY OF NEUTRALITY:

AN ADDRESS DELIVERED AT LOUISVILLE, KY., JULY 13TH, BY HON. JOSEPH HOLT; ALSO HIS LETTER TO J. F. SPEED, ESQ.

12mo., uniform with Everett's Oration. Price, 10 cents.

V.

NAPOLEON'S MAXIMS OF WAR: A MANUAL FOR OFFICERS.

RECOMMENDATION

"After refreshing my memory by looking over again 'The Officer's Manual,' or 'Maxims of Napoleon,' I think I may safely recommend the republication, in America, of the work in English, as likely to be called for by many officers, regular and volunteer. It contains a circle of maxims deduced from the highest source of military science and experience, with practical illustrations of the principles taken from the most celebrated campaigns of modern times. The study of the book cannot fail to set all young officers on a course of inquiry and reflection greatly to their improvement.

"WINFIELD SCOTT."

This little volume is of service and interest to the officer, the soldier, the civilian, and to all interested in the art of war.

One neat pocket volume, flexible cover. Price, 30 cents.

JAMES G. GREGORY, PUBLISHER,
(SUCCESSOR TO W. A. TOWNSEND & CO.,)
NO. 46 WALKER ST., N. Y.

IN PRESS.

PATRIOTIC AND HEROIC ELOQUENCE: A Volume of Prose and Poetical Extracts from the Speeches and Writings of Distinguished Men. 12mo., Cloth. Price, 75 cents.

C. A. ALVORD, PRINTER.

www.ingramcontent.com/pod-product-compliance
Lightning Source LLC
LaVergne TN
LVHW020644110826
845149LV00004B/1348

* 9 7 8 1 4 1 8 1 8 9 4 3 3 *